Anathematic Darkness

by Tom Cintula

ANATHEMATIC DARKNESS

© 2023 Tom Cintula. All rights reserved. No part of this book may be copied, reproduced or transmitted by any means without prior permission of the author, except in the case of brief quotations embodied in review articles.

Cataloguing-in-Publication entry is available from the National Library of Australia http:/catalogue.nla.gov.au/.

This edition first published in Hackham, South Australia by Immortalise via Ingram Spark in May 2023
www.immortalise.com.au

ISBN paperback 978-0-6457721-8-0
ebook 978-0-6457720-8-1

Typesetting and cover layout by Ben Morton
Cover image: Finsternis Natur by Elmar Ersch 2009 - sourced from Wikimedia Commons

Contents

1. The Wanderer 1
2. Scowl For A Mask 3
3. Your Decisions Are Your Family 6
4. Tears of Blood Lead To Broken Walls Of Doom 8
5. Utopias Are Boring 10
6. Feeling Numb Isn't Really Numb 12
7. Traveling With A Heavy Heart 14
8. Damaged Goods 15
9. Inhaling Pain, Exhaling Fire 17
10. My Mind Becomes My Compass 19
11. My Heartstrings And Soul Become My Water And Wine 21
12. Wanting To Die, Having To Live 23
13. Reform Yourself Only To Die Quicker 25
14. Anger 27
15. The Summer Tundra 29
16. Breathing Smoke 32
17. Fear Is Always There, But Don't Pay Too Much Attention To It 34
18. Life As It Is 36
19. Health Insurance In The US In A Nutshell 38
20. Hardiness 40
21. The Angry Doppelganger 42
22. You Get Out What You Put In 44
23. No Place To Go 46
24. Insanity Grants Serenity 48
25. Working For Purification 50
26. Swamped 52
27. Life, As We Know It 54
28. It's Hard To Breathe 56
29. Deep Feeler 58
30. Mission of Freedom 61
31. Tough Hate 63
32. Fist Of Fear 64
33. Identity Crisis 66
34. Fighting Against The Winds Of Dogma 68
35. Chill Pill 70
36. Getting Out Of Dodge 72
37. Controlled By Devils Of Madness 74
38. Nights Of Loneliness 76
39. People Can't Be Trusted 78
40. Die Before You Live 80
41. The Price Of Hardiness 82
42. Heart And Soul 84
43. The Fires Of Hell 86
44. An Event Like Any Other 88
45. Ill Affects Of Vitriol 90

46. Hello, I Love You 92
47. The Road To Anomaly... 94
48. Forgiveness: The Double-Edged Sword... 96
49. Shit Happens 98
50. Same Shit, Different Day... 100
51. My Heart: The Largest Muscle In My Body..................................... 102
52. Free In My Cocoon... 104
53. Going Boldly Where I Never Want To Go Again............................ 106
54. Arise From The Compost Of Hurt... 108
55. Bird's Eye View Of A Dystopia 109
56. Conscious While Unconscious 111
57. Youth Fades 113
58. Russian Roulette 115
59. Breaking News... 117
60. The Death Of Dystopia Depends On The People Who Build One.................. 119
61. What Do You Want To Be When You Pass On?............................ 120
62. Being And Doing... 122
63. Resetting The Table 124
64. My Brain Works, But My Mind Doesn't 126
65. The Fear Of Having Fear... 128
66. Soft Isn't Always Strong... 130
67. Comfort 132
68. Heatwave 134
69. Rambunctious Feelings 136
70. The Repression We Carry.. 138
71. Stuntman's High.. 140
72. R&R Should Be The Devil's Workshop.. 142
73. The Social Maze.. 144
74. Start Living Or Keep Dying... 146
75. Unkemptness = Control... 148
76. Feast Or Famine.. 150
77. Death Comes With Life... 152
78. Nobody's Perfect, But Complete 153
79. Outta Love, Outta Sight, Outta Mind.. 155
80. Journey Of A Swollen Heart... 157
81. Dreams And Nightmares.. 159
82. Fear Looking For A Friend 161
83. My Last Week Of Summer In Elkton... 163
84. Spoken Words of Wonder 165
85. Five Finger Discount Of Utopia 167
86. Ramble Poem About Liberation... 169
87. Either/Or.. 171
88. Hunger And Will Meets Solace... 173
89. Separating Man From Animal.. 175
90. In The Waiting Room For Death.. 177
91. Decades Of Anathematic Darkness.. 179

1. The Wanderer

    Wandering on the Island
    is like swimming in the dark,
    I'm kickin' your feet,
    treadin' water,
    but I don't know
    where you're goin'
    sometimes.

    Sometimes it's a wonder
    in itself to explore
    the borough, only to know
    that nobody cares that I exist.

    For instance, taking the bus
    with air conditioning on one end,
    but babies screaming, mothers
    screaming at them to shut up and
    sit down, slapping them in the face,
    only so they could cry and scream
    some more, on the other hand... literally.

    Reminds me of the time
    my mom was scolding me to sit down,
    only she didn't hit me, thank God.

    Sure, I lost my temper, but I didn't
    get hit, surprisingly.

    Beatin' the streets,
    sweatin' bullets at ninety-three,

degrees and tryin' to catch my breath
will have my mind
wandering about when
this road warrior voyage
will end.

This is considered training camp
in preparing for the vagabond
lifestyle, considering this is only
running errands to take a drug test
for a new job to ensure I'm
not a liability.

No car, but no problem,
but I have to do this,
rain or shine,
groggy or perky,
running around to piece
together a professional identity,
not only about who I am,
but I am where I go.

Ridin' the buses,
poundin' the pavement,
ferry freestylin'
hittin' the clubs,
divin' into the dives
headfirst into the
fire breathing crowd
to relieve me of the ever so
sweltering heat makes me
feel like I just ran a marathon.

2. Scowl For A Mask

A scowl is nothing more
than a mask covering
my fear from this
haunted universe.

I don't want anyone
to know how afraid I am,
so I fight instead of flight,
sometimes without even
fighting.

It doesn't mean
that I'm angry,
but it's a shield
to keep the vultures
at bay so I can
keep the peace in my heart,
only should I try to
spread it will make me
even easier prey.

Sometimes, though, I act
as if I'm angry, even if
I'm not and I even yell to
ensure that it's just an act,
but is it?

As for the scowl, it's my
shield while the words
I howl are my swords,

knives, and daggers.

As I wrinkle my forehead,
showing off my piercing stare,
my heart is beating faster
than I can get outta Dodge
from those very vultures.

That's me putting up
my shield with my sword
cocked behind me,
ready to strike.

Bottom line is, to get out
before I have to run
while going through
bodies chasing me
into the night and,
escape what death
has in store for me
with little time I have
until I die in vain…

which is even a minor
jab at my dignity all
because I have to pass
by the hallway just to
get to class or make it
through the day without
anyone saying anything
to me, good or bad.

Even a death stare can't
make the Reaper run

away from trying to kill me
and even if I fight back,
it's time to start digging
for a place to sleep.

All these pairs of eyes,
regardless of how many
people are watching me,
whispering a giggle or
even whispering a
profanity.

Meanwhile, my face is
mad, but my insides
are ridden with fear
and doom, even when
I look like death
itself walking down
the hallway of dark
jocularity.

3. Your Decisions Are Your Family

Indecisiveness is not weak,
as it is the mother of inner conflict.
Should I exercise today?
Should I go for a walk?
Should I eat now or later tonight?
Should I lay around and do nothing?
Or should I find something to do?
I'm not even sure if I should
sit in this chair and breathe.

Breathe, yes…

Sit…I'm not so sure,
maybe…
maybe not.

When ideas begin
to appear in my mind,
it's a world of what you do
once you choose to do it.

It becomes your family,
your bride and children,
your house to live in,
your bed to sleep in,
your toilet to sit on,
your shit to lay on.

It's your parole officer,
checking on you,

making sure you don't
backslide to what you
used to be and what
you're afraid to return
to being again.

The things you want to do
become the things you have
to do each and every day.

Like working out when you
don't want to, or going shopping
for the week when you can just
go straight home and do it
tomorrow.

Taking one more bus with
a load of loud passengers
sitting down while you're
standing for twenty minutes
more weakens the limbs
further while strengthening
the mind, saying,
"Only a little further to go before
we can go home and pass out."

That's the evolutionary essence
building its muscles when we
don't feel like it.

4. Tears of Blood Lead To Broken Walls Of Doom

Tears are a warm liquid
that can melt your heart
while rolling down your face.

It hurts to feel them
on your face more than
it does to deprive yourself
of what you need to feel.

It's almost like acid burning
your skin, only you're not hurt
by the tears, but the fact that
you've produced them.

And the fact that people get
to witness your pain in public
with a nosy, blank stare makes
it hurt even more, which works
our tear ducts into overdrive.

Hearts are broken each day
while souls bleed out and
minds shut down to process
the grief that you receive.

This puts life on pause, even if
the clock is ticking and you're
trying to collect yourself and
all those eyes are watching you.

Even better, if you're a young
professional in the city and you
have colleagues just laser-beam
stare you down while you're
running for the bathroom,
you're already compromised.

Your heart throbs of hurt
so intense that your soul
may disappear from the
exhaustion of your body's
response to being attacked.

Sometimes there is no
way to comprehend how
to bleed tears and
die on the inside.

If you cry, you cry, but your
insides become fragments
of what you had to protect
who you really are and the
walls which are shattered
are a passage to emotional
salvation, giving you the
freedom to profusely
writhe in the darkness
with no angels around
to catch you when you
fall.

5. Utopias Are Boring

I don't believe how I feel
about this world right now.
This place is a zoo...a total zoo.

A place where we fight, hate, growl,
and feud until we wear ourselves out
hammering away over things
which matter and things which don't.

Do you really want to fight me
over a seat on the bus with only
three people riding on it and
there are forty more seats
available for you to sit in?

Fuck you!

Fuck you, but take my seat.
There's probably a better
place to sit anyway.

By the way, isn't that
how Cliff Burton died?

Anyway, fighting over as much as a
parking spot, a piece of bread,
a woman's affections,
or just to be heard is a job
without recognition,
let alone compensation...

or do they both intertwine?

Some people, just have to scrap
only to get out of bed, let alone
work for a day, just to buy a
Red Bull to keep them up for
at least a few more hours.

We work too hard,
hate too much,
and love too little,
which is when…
that's a good time to let go,
forget about this place,
this dystopia that
we all live in,
that if it were
a utopia,
we would be bored.

There would be so much
serenity where hot air and
burning passions would
reside, only to be trapped
behind a veneer of happiness,
finding us with our brains
splattered on the living room
rug, under the dining room
table, and blood trickling
into the kitchen.

6. Feeling Numb Isn't Really Numb

I don't believe how I feel
about this world right now.

How do I feel all of this if I'm numb?
When I'm numb, I can still feel, right?
What kind of human being does this make me?
How do I know how to feel if everything is numb?

I'm not sure I want to feel,
because it's sweet and sour sauce
in my stomach every day.

It's an ebb and flow that
can be most uncomfortable,
even if it's a good feeling.

Feelings will dominate you,
even if you don't act on them,
not because you're afraid to,
but because they hurt.

Even if you're feeling great
about a raise you got,
it's not like you're gonna be rich.

Even if you bought a new car,
it's not like it's gonna stay new.

Even if you just got married,
your significant other probably

got married earlier before they
decided to marry you, who knows?

It's a hard-soft combination,
killing everything that
haunts me inside of me
while I marinate
in the sweet and sour,
which is the hard and soft,
fighting those haunting me
recklessly hard only to kill
with the caressing of their souls
as its fatality.

Imperiled with a fortitude
so hardened by this planet,
even without traveling throughout,
it would take only a tanginess
followed by a spritz of bitterness
to cure the conditioning that
only a brick wall can consume.

Feels like a rough block of
cement filling my nerves with
nothingness.

7. Traveling With A Heavy Heart

My heart is heavy
all because it's hard as
this boulder I carry shaped
just like one and guts made
straight out of concrete
with my veins becoming
boiled with anger,
all due to the hardiness
I take with me everywhere
I go.

How do I not look
like Ronnie Coleman
carrying this weight inside
of me when I don't want to?

It's hard to carry a heart
which doesn't beat,
but at least I got heart, right?

How does one build character
carrying something with them
they didn't choose to,
especially if it's just as bad
as Jesus carrying his cross
just before he gets nailed
to it?

8. Damaged Goods

Microaggressions are
small seeds of
pain inflicted on
all of us when we
least expect it.

It's like a walk in the park
before it becomes a
stroll in the city at night
with a nervous heart,
beating rapidly and
rambunctiously,
looking around for
death hiding behind the bushes
to stab you from behind.

Or like a stranger in the night
that pricks you on the side
and then runs right off before
he attacks another
pedestrian.

Or like a bee who stings you
on the arm or shoulder
with the venom
lodged in your bloodstream.

They're not too bad,
but they're not too good
because a pinch, a scratch,

a flick of the ear,
a scrap of the knee,
a stub of a toe,
a snide remark
accumulate to deeper
waters and uncharted
territories of doom.

Add 'em all up and
with the right math,
you have…damaged goods.

9. Inhaling Pain, Exhaling Fire

Living in your own mind
is a whole different world
from the world you're
supposed to live in.

It's fun, free, adventurous,
but the adventure is worth it,
because it's a dream that
you have in your mind.

Just imagine hang gliding
into outer space with no
escape while cracked
out of your mind.

In reality, you're dying
slowly, but living with
a purpose to stay alive,
which causes you to
breathe life into yourself.

Puff out the pain and
insert the fire into your soul
to spit out at the world.

Just cool off every once
in a while and swim
into your paradise,
but travel into your
dreams during the day
and live there for a while.

When you live in your
own mind, you live in
a world that you can't
only see, but you want
the rest of it to see.

Puff out the pain and
insert the fire into your soul
to spit out at the world.

Breathe out the smoke for others
to witness how disgruntlement
works for you so you can overthrow
dystopia and fill the fresh air
with the disenfranchisement
you possess to melt the cynicism
that the world has carried with
them for far too long.

Puff out the pain and
insert the fire into your soul
to spit out at the world.

Make sure the fire burns down
the blackness caused by natural
and universal disasters and pain
that follows afterwards.

10. My Mind Becomes My Compass

My mind is spinning
like a washing machine
and dryer, going around
in circles that make me
dizzy when my eyes roll
into the back of my head.

Out of my mind and
into a world of confusion,
I can't seem to find where
I am, searching for a way out
of this only to lose direction,
to escape the radar and
disappear.

It's me vanishing while on
the radar and then vanishing
while off into thin air.

I need a compass to keep up
with the way my mind
makes me travel, as my
indecisiveness takes me
to far away lands,
mysterious worlds
never visited before in my life.

Deserts, abandoned crackhouses,
underdeveloped planets.
padlocked diners,

boarded skid shacks,
old delis with outdated
food, which makes me
think, "Wow! I need to get out
more than ever!"

This is the utopia the
media needs to champion
more often.

I guess my mind IS
my compass.

11. My Heartstrings And Soul Become My Water And Wine

My heartstrings and soul
have a part which galvanize
my spirit to feel the burn
of the world I suffer from.

Like acid, only no one wants
to tell me, as it puts a hole into
my spirit, igniting an early
death for all to see, yet I still
get to live with this inside me.

Interconnected like water and wine,
there's always something that
strikes the chords when I feel.

A name, a dirty look,
a clenched fist,
something that draws an ire
causing the beast within me
to stay on caution for a fight
that you're afraid to have.

But the fights you don't want,
are the ones you need the most.

I hate to admit it,
but it's required…

Yeah, I'm sorry, man,

but don't worry so much,
'cuz once it's over,
win or lose, you'll feel
a lot better about fighting.

Go with the guts you have
and act abrasively…
it might be accordingly.

My heartstrings and soul
become my water and wine,
which is equal to my spirit.

12. Wanting To Die, Having To Live

Everywhere you go,
there's always someone
that's dying inside from
being lovelorn, stressed,
bitter, feeling forced to
self-loathe and hate
themselves and wishing
to die.

Wanting to die,
yet staying alive is
nothing more than a
magic trick we all do.

Like asking for love,
but receiving hate instead.

You wish you could, but
choose to stay alive
just to see how much
farther you can go
before your tolerance
for life begins to decline.

That's when it's gut check time
to see if you want to keep
living only to die
from the inside out.

You want to die.

You want to kill yourself.
You want to think you're
ready for death, even when
you know you're not.

You're dying, all right,
but it's slow and emotionally
painful enough to give you
the time to build resistance
against the roughness of
the real world and what
media sells to you once
you persevere.

Maybe you should go ahead
apply for that coveted firearm
license only to turn it onto
yourself.

Make sure you're ready,
willing, and able.

13. Reform Yourself Only To Die Quicker

I ran from the hurt
that continues to follow me
while wanting to hurt those
who don't deserve it as they
can't suspect one to want to
eat them alive,
when I don't have it
in me to do it when
I know that I should,
but only to the right people.

I'm aching everywhere,
but in my mind
where I think about setting
the world ablaze only to
exhibit restraint well enough
to become invisible.

When I disappear, though,
make sure I never come back,
because if I do,
I'll just kill you…

I mean I'll just fuckin' kill you.

I will absolutely make sure that
I never have to live with the regret
of being afraid of you or even
the regret of letting you harm me
in any way possible because

my rage is so high for you
that I have to kill you.

I didn't know how to fight,
but I know how to kill now,
thanks to being bitter,
which is justified.

As long as there aren't any
witnesses, it's in the middle
of the night, and I'm
absolutely one hundred
percent confident I can
get away with it and I
don't ever return to that
scene of the crime again,
count me in.

Make sure I don't kill you,
but if I do, just make sure
you're reformed so
I can kill you easier.

14. Anger

It hurts more to be angry
than it does to be sad, sometimes.
Anger hurts the soul and
wears me out a lot,
affecting the heart
and filling it up with stress.

I feel the need to scream
where my emotions must
be expelled from this
anatomy, tensed up with
an energy that matches
my fire and fills the
void I need filled
to breathe life into
this dead, fading world.

Sadness makes you droopy,
flaccid, and looking like
Eeyore all the time,
but anger keeps you tense
and upright to a point
where you're headed for
a world of hypertension
so high, you'll die just
looking at a salt shaker,
whether or not it carries
salt.

When you're upset or

angry, fuming a temper
tantrum that no one else
wants to see, you're probably
burning more calories
doing that than working
out in the gym.

15. The Summer Tundra

Sitting at the bar,
sucking on a soda while
taking in the air conditioner
is the only sense
of happiness that I'll
ever have for today.

The arctic atmosphere is
the stillness that freezes
up my perspiration,
chilling away the heat
I brought with me to
the restaurant.

Pretty soon, I can see
my own breath
as the AC blowing
gives me a vision of a tundra
manageable to radiate.

I can't believe that I
remember going to this
bar at eight-thirty a.m. after
a long night working
at Pathmark and throw
down a Keystone
that would get
me buzzed while the AC
was on, giving me the
comfort of a nurturing

mother that the sweltering
heat of a punishing father
can usually bring.

It's a feeling that brings me
back to a wintry scene in July,
as whiteness represents
darkness through snow,
cold breezes blowing into
the bar, icicles around the
window sill outside, and the
sun shining through the
clouds while there's nothing
to shine about because it's
a sad, cloudy wintry weekend.

The TV is showing some
newscast and everyone's lined
up, sitting at the bar,
numbing their souls with
alcohol, but I'm wondering
if this is too good to be true,
where doing this at home
will cost me less, only I'm
in worse company than
I would be alone.

I just wanna get away from
the loneliness I've been
spoiled with just to
feel more utterly worthless
sitting with patrons I'm
afraid to meet, as they
munch on meat and drink

themselves back to when
they could house down
a thousand ounces of alcohol
to house down six hundred,
embellishing the amount.

Like trading a Lamborghini
for a beat up old Volvo
with hood racks on top,
I'll just walk home in
the cold, I mean,
I got my thermals on
and all, but if the heater
runs and not the car,
I ain't drivin' it.

I'm still hot, though, even
when I'm sitting in the
bar, rubbing my arms
instead of my chest,
the summer tundra
keeps me cool while
I'm still sweating.

Hot and cold intertwined.

16. Breathing Smoke

Smoke is an element
that helps you notice
somewhere in the air that
anger is beginning
to burn a hole in your stomach,
only to hurt you so bad
that your intestines
will boil while your mind
thinks about one thing…

Rage.

A beating heart is a sound
telling you to beat down
the walls around you
just to have a little
space to breathe a new form
of poetic justice into your soul…
freedom and living to be,
to do, to want, to fight,
to win, to lose, only to fight again,
but not even to win or lose,
but to live…and to die.

That's the ebb and flow
of breathing smoke,
feeling the burn inside,
but not seeing the smoke
come out of your ears
and mouth.

It sure feels hot inside, though
because when someone's
upset, sometimes, you feel
their fire, as well as the
hurt, which is marinated in
fire.

Even a sincere "hello"
can set them off.

That might be a form of
poetic justice into their
soul.

17. Fear Is Always There, But Don't Pay Too Much Attention To It

Fear is not just a four-letter word,
but a way of life and expression
for us to endure through the
misfortunes of their lesser
world of existence that
makes them wonder:
"Should we die in battle, or live
without fighting?"

Fear is a world, a being,
a trend,
a feeling that transcends our
livelihood,
but with a ball of heat
lit underneath our spirits
to storm the fearless,
as they are due to
their previous struggles
and choice to corrupt
those to assassinate
the beauty that the
world is missing.

When beauty and
aesthetics of the
simple things in life
are dead, we might
as well be.

Eating a watermelon
in the shower or
watchin' a game and
havin' a Bud prevent
us from being so.

Even stimming in front
of the computer screen,
rockin' back and forth,
watching Street Fight
Compilations 21 while
listening to Billy Joel.

Without that, what'cha
gonna do to even relax?!?

Ya know?!?

That in itself is a good way
to break away from the
fear that society brings
into our soul.

This helps us live
by fighting.

18. Life As It Is

Life is an event
that has only a limited
amount of time for us to
do what we want for us to
do what we want in only
any way we see fit,
where simply living and breathing
only adds to whatever
renegade status we all must
untap to release
in a big place where
living alone is
just not allowed.

Life, in its own right
is a full time stage
performance,
going to school,
work,
battle against your biggest arch rival…
yourself, all while facing your other rivals.

Whether the worldwide stage
we live on is round or flat,
it's more like a ring or mat
when it's land, air, fire,
or water that come together to create
the fireworks we see to
make this world go in circles
while your sanity travels

around it,
enculturing yourself
in a socioeconomic warfare
with even your own neighbors
that you don't care
even exist.

It's a trip of calamity
that will wear you out
while you act, laugh, cry,
lie, bare your soul,
and solve your problems
while more are on deck to
hit you into the stars,
falling among them
while reaching for the moon,
only to be owned by the sun.

19. Health Insurance In The US In A Nutshell

Heading to the pharmacy,
ready to pick up my
prescriptions,
only to discover that I
have to pay $623 for
an inhaler to aid
my respiratory issues.
All the hackin',
wheezin', throat clearin'
hard swallowin' times
where I have to
wait until my throat
is a hundred percent clear
for twenty minutes to
an hour where I can't
relax until my
throat is pristine.

How many people
can raise their hand
in unison and say
that they had the
same thing happens to them?

Rushing to the pharmacy,
only to discover that
your carrier won't pay
jack squat for you to
feel better when you
need that special something

to do so, only you have to
pay out of pocket while
carrying Medicaid?

My insurance doesn't mean
shit to anyone who
"knows how I feel"
anymore and no matter
how they say it,
they will never know what it's
gonna be like to have insurance
that won't help you when
you need it the most.

No one cares about the
people who struggle or
give a shit when others don't
about anything like this,
I mean,
anyone else goes
through this bullshit?

20. Hardiness

Hardiness is an intangible
that can wear you AND
me right out while trying
to merely exist in this world,
breathing, sweating,
working, living,
which cause us all to die,
with the addiction
of the scars we collect
on the way to our graves,
or unless we get cremated.

Or…
it'll just blow away into the air
then, which is better than a
swarm of bees chasing us
up and down the street.

Otherwise,
even an ounce of that
always gets us out of bed,
gets the job done,
helps those in need,
and may give us a view
of a better future.

Hardiness is quite the
intangible that gives us
an interphysical battle
inside of us where we're

psyched and ready to go
into the actual battle
against the guy you're
auditioning against,
fighting against across
the cage, or sometimes
the person who's about
to be accepted into your
dream school by a
hundredth of a point
and you don't even know
who they are or what
they even look like.

Hardiness means we want
whatever we want so bad
that it pumps us up to a
level of getting it by force.

We must cling our inner animal
and then thrust it against the air
into the matter, endure, refang,
endure, refang, endure, and then
refang some more.

That's what wins any type of war.

Whatever mountain you make
out of that molehill, builds the
hardiness into a castle with an
underground dungeon made up
of a jungle seen in Africa.

Brace yourself the way Stu braced

his boys for battle, only against
the rest of the universe.

21. The Angry Doppelganger

The need for anger is
a hunger that we want to
be able to control,
even though sometimes
we must be able to explode,
where our rage is a
security blanket
to keep us warm, safe,
and sound.

Anger scares me to a point
where I'm more afraid
while angry,
even though I don't
want to be,
as fear comes out from not
wanting to fight to
having to in order not to
be afraid of adversaries,
such as life in general and its
protectors who keep it
miserable for those who
want to live and let live.

Fighting scares me badly,
but I know someday...
somethin's a brewin'
where I'm gonna fight
someone that I can't beat
that just has to lose.

Not just because they have to,
but because I have to beat
them for myself.

Sometimes, that's the best
way to have closure.

But who will it be…and why?

22. You Get Out What You Put In

Everyday is a chance for
us to live more happily
than we normally do,
only to be surprised by
what we receive from
the things we do.

We learn how much
more we have to do
just to live with the
contentment we've earned
after all we've given life as
we expect life to give to us.

When life takes things away
from you, though, it's a time
to find something new where
it won't leave you,
just don't
leave it either.

No matter what we give
nor what we get back,
we have ourselves at the end
and what we've acquired to
further develop what we've
become and morphed into
at the end of it all.

For instance, you acquire

the knowledge to learn the streets,
you could either become
a junkie or a drug kingpin.

Or if you acquire the abilities to
become a...professional wrestler
by going to a wrestling facility,
training three or four nights
a week for a year and a half,
learn to work a crowd,
execute the maneuvers safely
and correctly before you
travel statewide and then
out of state to wrestle without
missing a show, get sore, hurt,
and seriously injured, fucked with,
beat up a lot, told that you suck
a lot, told that you don't draw
flies to a shit factory
drive across the country,
wrestle literally everywhere,
get promised to be pushed
only to be held down by the
powers that be, get hurt by
some idiot who doesn't know
what the fuck they're doing,
and gets your push instead,
you become...bitter.

You get out what you put in.

23. No Place To Go

Sometimes, I wish I wasn't so angry,
as the fury I have isn't something
that I hold onto as much as
it's holding onto me,
but only tighter.

That fury is a lifetime of
darkness that lived inside
of me to become the depression
that people began to notice about
me, leaving me alone to protect
their own feelings while others
were drawn to it to make me
feel worse, sucking my already
drained energy to have more
for themselves to get through
the day faster.

Then when the depression
disappears and the emotions
change rapidly, the fire ignites
into a hot sun, boiling me up
enough to punch a wall or
a locker.

Angry enough to react,
scared enough to confront
the enemy.

I can't stand how I feel

where my frustration becomes
a world that can't contain
what I have inside me.

Branching out with my
brains scattered on the
bedroom floor, wall,
and mattress would've
been the ticket out
of this world into
a sea of black or
maybe a lake of fire.

Anger is a stress that's
worse than exerting
yourself in a gym
or garden,
or even going to work,
unless you're angry there too.

There are people that are, but
the benefits, colleagues, and
Manager King Shit keeps us
in line each day, which makes us
even angrier.

It's a pain that hurts
and makes you feel like
you're walking in the desert,
sweaty and beat to the ground,
perspiring,
only to melt under the sun.

24. Insanity Grants Serenity

I resume on a road of
tension to drive on,
giving me the world
in front of me that I
must live into provide in
a universe of my own where
I must live to thrive,
If not survive,
but to live without walls
or mirrors…
To live without traffic signs,
To live without coaches,
To live without parents,
To live without a conscience,
like choosing not to shower,
or wearing undergarments
underneath your clothing.

How about walking out
of the house with no clothes
on, letting yourself go into
the street, with every vehicle
waiting for the light to turn green
only to see you prance around
in the nude with no Jaguar
or Dodge to hide into while
the rest of them have to pay
off those leases to keep those
cars and that means for them
not to walk around, liver spots

and all, giving life the big bird,
doin' the La Parka in the
median of the freeway.

Just to live how you want
and however you can,
even if you're not allowed,
you still are…
Grant yourself
freedom of bitterness.

The serenity to exert the
darkness is the key to sanity.

25. Working For Purification

Day in, day out
there's always something,
where over my exertion is an
adventure, where like
the rest of humanity,
working beyond belief
to preserve life,
just to be able to have the honor
of living it with a slice of
free will and a chunk of determinism,
only to end up having
nothing to be
necessarily proud of overall.

Scrambling is the only option that
most people have just to live,
while they shouldn't,
but due to forces outside
their proverbial control,
grinding only to obtain meaning,
and sad enough, an occupation
gives them that meaning.

Everyone has some sort of
prestigious title or another
identity that they're being
referred to in order to have
some sort of meaning in
their lives, scraping enough
only to realize they'll

have to work longer and
harder, only to live in
meat scraps and drown in
self-pity, given the fact that
dreaming big and aiming high
results in destruction for a lot
of us, giving us a chance to
start over only to land a gig
serving the world for nothing
while trying to rectify a battered
soul with a hobby in order to
purify it.

Good luck.

26. Swamped

To look around me and see
people grow up to become
what the world gunpoints us
to become can scare anyone,
but only with a glare,
snarl, or an idle threat
strong enough.

Everyone I know today
has ownership of their lives,
but do they really if they're
living with the herd as their
nightwatcher to do what each
generation has done before,
which is produce, reproduce,
obey and conform where I,
who lives with no boundaries,
that no one knows or cares that
if I live or die, have evolved
with a mind spinning like a top
and your insides bleed in
sour doses of dreams of gold
now settling into private suffering
and anonymity where only I
can sort out the pieces one by one.

To privately suffer is to ask
yourself, "What have I done?",
all while you're home from a
job you don't like and you have

children racing each other to
get to you first, only to be
too tired to hug them, let alone
play hide-and-seek with them.

The child in you is dead,
and the soul is recovering
from the pounding it took
from virtually everyone,
but when you rest your
head on the pillow upstairs,
you're just as lonely as you
are alone, recharging from
the spiritual sweating you
enduring the lashes the
week gives you.

That's from obeying the
norms we were tricked into
believing would give us
"peace of mind" when
we only get it from
sleeping those problems away,
escaping into the abyss of
the fantasies we have of
another life that will
never happen.

27. Life, As We Know It

Life, as we know it,
is a happening that
all of us live in to determine
who, where, and what we're going to be.

We live on borrowed time,
exploring ourselves
in this big world
with so much to offer,
yet so little that we've
accomplished no matter how much
we tried to will our way
to live with security
but instead,
we fall hard into a pit
of pity as our universal system
deprives us of merely
breathing sometimes.

Yet we've gained enough wisdom
not to be philosopher kings,
but we all understand that we
all can't be chosen.

Forget about your failed dreams,
try struggling to breathe more
life into this world while
trying to stay alive in defiance
of a herd that watches you
die from the inside out with

a beer in one hand and
popcorn in another.

So what if you were gonna be
the next great ballerina,
rock star or basketball god.

Even if you do what you love,
you're not going to be happy anyway
because people want you to fail,
even drop dead while doing
what you love.

Everyone is trapped in a
world suffocating us
from existence forces us
to revolt so we can stay alive
in a world that shapes us,
yet doesn't want us.

Make them want you
or tell them to fuck off!

28. It's Hard To Breathe

There are holes in my stomach
while I maintain a
beating unstill heart,
and an anatomy in need
to unleash hordes of air.

Thing is, the holes
bleed winds of pain
stemming from the anger
caused by the social animals
who helped with this.

They've drained me to the
point where my soul disappears
and my blood thins out into air.

This can only mean one thing…
I'm trapped in panic,
where my guts are hurting
to the point of stagnancy.
As I fawn in my bed,
breathing second by second,
I bare a soreness that
may be too painful for me
to breathe in and out.

It's like a fist lodged inside
of my stomach,
where gagging is more
of a thing than breathing,

if only my tender intestines
can further withstand the
writhing aches of this episodic
attack, maybe, just maybe,
I'll be a stronger man,
only to go through the motion
with a sharper psyche
before it becomes duller.

Otherwise, everything starts to go
when I exhibit this pain, dying
far too slowly trying to breathe,
only to gag enough to die when
I don't want to.

Problem is I want to die
but I have to wait until
the right time,
even though I'm
ready now.

29. Deep Feeler

When I feel, I live a life
most people can't imagine,
as when I laugh, I live
in a comedy where the joke
takes me to a world that
laughs along with me.

It takes me to a place
where it's funny to
see yourself trip on a curb
and split your head open,
laughing while picking your
brains up off the sidewalk
and carry them to the
bus stop to wait for
the bus to pick you up
while they're on your lap.

When I exhibit hurt feelings,
I experience a knife
that cuts me deep enough to
double over in staggering pain,
absorbing shock from the blow
with the point sticking out my back
feeling the blood drip down my spine
to hear it drop onto the floor.

When I get mad,
I take on a world where
I'm burning up inside

while burning calories
yelling, screaming,
and getting into a fight,
but only with myself,
only scared to fight others.

As for confusion, my mind spins fast
and speaks louder than any person
standing behind a microphone as
I can see my thoughts being filmed
in a studio.

When I suffer anxiety,
the world becomes bigger,
taller, wider, darker,
and more of a maze
with no end point in sight.

The buildings erect even larger,
the doorways close in,
and the lights get more dim
with the switch on.

When I feel heavy,
lethargic, and faint,
I end up weighing
more than a hundred
buckets of water where
I have to carry each one
everywhere I go.

My life, is an
adventure where
I can't escape, whether

a fantasy or real life
that I live inside,
looking for a way out
only to be forced to live
while praying for a
trap door to come
and open itself
underneath my feet
so I can fall into a
ready-made grave
that turns out to
be a bottomless pit.

This double life that
I've lived in has given
me the ability to
travel to places most
people will never dare
to go to, almost to a point
where the entire world,
alone is an escape in of
itself from the world
that most will never
know that exists.

30. Mission of Freedom

Living isn't just a notion
that we have just to have,
but an investment in who we are,
what we do, where we go,
among all the things to choose from,
or that choose us that fulfill us,
bastardize us, guide us,
and make us see what type of
world we have in store for us.

That obstacle course in front of us
gives us a life to see that will
open us up to an anguish which
should sicken us so much
we must start our own while
watching this one obliterate us,
giving citizens a life to live,
only to die with a crapshoot
of being remembered or
forgotten.

With that said, having an
obituary written in the newspaper,
reviewing our lives makes
us famous for a brief moment,
but our presence immortalize
us in a societal sea of mortals
keeping our planet as one.

We go through each day hurdling

over obstacle after obstacle,
be it waking up early enough
to catch the bus for work or
social and psychological
warfare against the hucksters
that scorn us day in and day out
we actually ride with on those
very buses or just trying to
stay sane in a dark world
looking to provoke us to
join the herd of darkness.

To retire our soul to the herd
of darkness is to live for
the good of the evil and
desecrate the masses of
the good to make them
suffer, starve, and die
without actualization.

We must live with the notion
of exhibiting the freedom
to give us all power to
want less and use our
mortality to immortalize us
without the consent of the elites
or outside forces.

Our mission is clear, but
we must make it visible.

31. Tough Hate

Every time I wake up
in the morning to start
off my day, my guts
hurt with the soreness
of an empty stomach,
as if they've been taken
out of me or melted by
the fear that lies ahead
for me.

Where I feel it, the soul
cries for some food.

Sometimes, it cries for a Xanax.
I end up anticipating more than
what the unknown has
in store for me as
the lingering worm that
lurks inside of me, penetrating
through every layer to try
to eat my soul while I
withstand a morning of
uncertainty.

Somehow, I manage to
get up and walk through the
ice picks that I can't see,
enduring my life with
each step I take and with
each word that I utter,

only to be gored each day,
building the resistance to live
through the sharpness of life's itinerary…
tough hate.

32. Fist Of Fear

When my body feels
a throb and a shake
as my mind wakes me
up with a past of tantrums,
trauma with added beastly emotions
and its hideous feelings, making me
tremble deep inside sending
shockwaves all around me.

On nights where I wake up
carrying these feelings
and holding my stomach
for collecting every ounce of
anxiousness, nervousness,
catastrophic wonder of the rest of my life,
with constant curiosities of
this evolving environment
that we remain we roam in
that will constantly psych us all out,
only for us to form a mindset
that everything is finite
and our ingenuity for survival
is truly infinite.

My equilibrium is a pendulum
swinging like a marauder swinging
an axe, aimlessly headhunting
with a wonder whether or not
they'll find solace with a
beheading just like I wonder

if I'll find solace beheading
my own anxiety.

Either a pill can cut through my
fear and shred it up or my guts
get crushed by a fist of fear.

33. Identity Crisis

Living on Earth is always trivial,
wondering where we stand,
what we want, but above all,
what we don't want.

All of us are alive, but
not always well
carrying ourselves into each day,
looking into ourselves
with open eyes and an
open mind, searching for a
future with wonder and
in seeking for something
that is real inside of us.

No matter how real
things look to everyone,
we have all overlooked
the authenticity that our
land has concealed from
us instead of taking the time
to investigate what this
life is, not by living freely,
but by wondering why
the corrupt and powerful
life more freely than those
who make with what they can
with the little that they have.

Finding your fit for how to live

takes us through so many archetypes
that most of us must undergo to
find the right self that help us live
as defiantly as we must all learn how.

As chameleons, we still remain in
the form of a human while morphing
into different people to survive,
realizing we must retain our
true selves playing someone else.

34. Fighting Against The Winds Of Dogma

Heart is the last thing
people think about when
it comes to sealing victory
because all they want
to do is dominate,
destroy, and not be denied
until something drastic
happens to them.

They get hit, maybe not drilled
or hit as hard as it would look,
but once that happens, doubt
begins to seep in quickly.

Where they should fight harder
to destroy it, doubt quickly spreads
worse than a virus or a disease
throughout the mind, body, and
soul, where fear finds a special
place in our hearts.

No one needs help to bully others,
but everyone needs help to combat
bullies, where we combat fear and
even rationality to understand the
true meaning of courage.

Courage, heart, and soul come
while trying to rationalize your
atmosphere while enduring the

beating you're taking while trying
to snap out of going where the wind
wants to take you.

It's time to transform into
the typhoon you were meant
to be, to blow back against the
winds of dogma and battle
yourself against the opponents
you're facing, not just the
opponents.

35. Chill Pill

Fatigue isn't when you can't
run another step anymore,
but when you can't run
with the same crowd anymore
when your interests change,
or when your world needs
a new variety or flavor.

It's when you get tired of
doing the same thing over and over
again that empty becomes a
screeching reality
with a spirit so beat
it sweats when your intestines
rumble and the tension slows you down.

The constant favors,
the cover ups and lies,
the toxic conversations
and pointless gossip
we have to sit around and
listen to every day.

Your feelings run on an
emotional treadmill
that has no off button
and it's in constant need
of a breather, where
the one suffering
needs to breathe with

air and space surrounding
them in a place where
they find touch with
the biggest strange
that they never
really met before…
themselves.

I could use a few Gatorades
to refuel or at least several days
to recharge where I can just
lie down and let the blood flow
through my body like a river valley
and my mind can play like a
television set when I can see
the beach, hear the waves,
squint at the seagulls, and
even the surfers riding
those thunderous waves
where the breeze is the
icing on a cake so
scrumptious, I can
never stop eating.

Therefore, I will never
stop taking in the rays,
tuning in to see summer
at peace, sharing its
serenity with me.

36. Getting Out Of Dodge

It's compromising to be helpful,
young, overwilling, and sacrificial,
but no one warns you about the
mistakes that you're going to make,
not because you're scanning
the world up and down,
but the world has a hit out for you.

All the excitement that you have just
brainstorming about dominating
the world makes you forget about
what the obstacle course of life
is all about and how much work
there is that's ahead just to eke through
each day where life is closing around
you.

Youth fleets away with each ounce of
grinding, with social construction,
working for scraps in general, finding ways
to make life more bearable when there's almost little money to
live on.

Adding to the mix,
living to feed a habit
that keeps you alive and happy,
whatever it is,
becomes the end game,
where our lives yearn
to stay alive.

Knowing we fill a void
in professions that
we choose because
we must sustain
what society cherishes
too dearly…
mediocrity.

37. Controlled By Devils Of Madness

I try to relax and
take a nap, just to feel my limbs
all tensed up and my jaw
hardened with each yawn,
stressed out with bloodshot eyes,
swimming in my sweat
while hoping to dream
with closed eyes and
a loud and active mind.

Maybe I'll wear myself out
tossing and turning,
but asleep or awake,
dead of alive,
daydreaming or in
hyperfocus,
my world is louder
than the reality that
I can't ignore.

That reality is the
restlessness ready to break
out of me like a skeleton
busting out of my skin,
jolting out of me with a
boyish rush, angst
of fury, and a craving
to be as uncontrollable
as could be, all while
being controlled by

the devils of madness.

The puppet masters of my
afterlife come to control me
to the point of exhaustion,
where I sweat blood to the
point where my autopilot
flies the frequent flier
mileage fast enough to
crash and burn while I
commit the same sins
over and over again.

Cursing and screaming,
trying over and over again
to run right through a brick wall,
hurling fists, flinging
trash cans in broad daylight,
chasing bums with a pickaxe,
diving into the drive-thru window
to chase after the Taco Bell employee
who stupidly forgot my chalupa
and Coke, driving after the scumbag
who cut me the fuck off before I
end up rear-ending a cop car,
becoming the chaos that I
envision in my mind is
the dream that comes true,
even if I don't want it to.

That's the thundering noise
only I can hear and I can stop
before it stops me from living
and starts becoming the

puppet master who halts
my dreams for stillness.

I guess I'll rest when I'm dead.

38. Nights Of Loneliness

On some nights, we are destined
to walk through, crisp, cool winds
with the music of traffic,
the beaming lights adding
color as a hustling-bustling day
ends in darkness,
but begins for the night owls of the world.

Those who walk down
the streets in solitude
from others, turn away
from the blinding brightness
of the day that melts their spirit
followed by the screaming
hyenas they come in contact with
that break them.

Other nights, we're destined to squint
while on a scavenger hunt for the light
in a path of loneliness, wondering
where the light is and whether or not
we're gonna bump into a tree or
get mugged by a bum.

All in all,
night is a time of
reflection that can
be our best friend,
soothing us
whether awake

or asleep.

It can be your
worst enemy
when you run
out of time
at day's end,
but its dark skies
bring a beauty
that outweighs
out planets wondrous
atmosphere that helps
us be still.

39. People Can't Be Trusted

Dealing with people
is a quizzical adventure,
where curiosity
is the one thing
that brings me to
the edge of my seat.

Who is this person?
Am I interested in them?
What do they want with me?
What do they want FOR me?
What do they want FROM me?

I can't relax nor forget
about what I need or want
to be so I don't lose
everything that I have.

For instance, energy from
the people who are
running low on it take it
from others to regain their
high because if a Clif Bar
or 5-Hour Energy doesn't do it,
sucking the morale out
of young souls'll do the trick.

It's better to pay
attention to yourself in
a conversation than the person

you're in contact with that
you can't trust.

Either their words
are hollow when
they speak to you
or your ears fail to pick up
their message.

You can't listen
to them nor
can they project
their symbol of
expression to you through
words.

Should you give them
the time of day
or shield yourself
from their words
which have no weight?

40. Die Before You Live

    Rising up is so
    much easier
    once your worst days
    have left you behind
    because the pressure's off.

    To be successful, rich or poor,
    all you have to do,
    mostly, is be willing to die
    over and over before you
    die again, where you become
    immune to destruction.

    Commit to the idea of
    inner death, emotional
    shutdown, psychological
    demotion, and mental crucifixion.

    Suck all you want,
    but suck in the poison
    given to you,
    so you can release it
    in a *tour de force*
    that will grant you
    your freedom,
    depending on what
    you decide.

    Suck it up with a straw
    and let the dust dissolve

into your bloodstream
to feel the lethal consumption
go down your gullet,
let it boil and roast them,
melting them down
with each drop until
they become a puddle
of matter.

Whether lethal or
sentimental,
brash or graceful,
one thing's for sure,
the setbacks that linger
inside of you,
bring power in
every action that
you take because
you're not gonna
lose forever,
that's for sure.

41. The Price Of Hardiness

Living with an
appealing hardiness
can save your life,
when those least
expect it.

When problems arise
and it forms to be
an injustice dealt,
rage mixed with heartache,
alongside deep confusion
will rocketfuel you to
go head on with
something to do
that must move you
to show purpose while
its purpose shows you
what can and must be
done to live on.

A diehard passion,
whether exhibited
loudly or quietly,
qualifies us to keep
this planet spinning
and depends on us to
save businesses with
our work that don't
save us through
their greed,

but we must
survive somehow
and that is how
our hardiness is used…
to save ourselves.

Hardiness can increase
lifelong vitality, but burn
you out and just as you
go upstairs to lie down
on your bed to go to sleep,
you'll fade away, melting
into the mattress, becoming so
in Daniel Day-Lewis-like
fashion.

Chill out…

42. Heart And Soul

Heart and soul
are more so
weapons than
intangibles
that live in us
so we can live
in vain to
revolt
against the
worthlessness
that media
tells us that
we are.

Lose weight,
buy this stock,
I wake up at
4 AM and don't
sleep 'till
2 AM the
next day,
if you live in
pain today,
you'll die
without it tomorrow,
and onward.

To live against
a conglomerate
filled with those

telling us what
to do will sell
the world ablaze,
one radical action
at a time
and that
conglomerate
is a herd of
shysters and
cheapskates.

If you want to go
do these things,
fine, but don't
depend on them
for too long as
the heart and soul
are the tools to
outweigh any
message sent
to make you
feel like you
have to change
what you know now.

Unlearning
will set you far more
free than joining a gym,
reading a self-help book,
or hiring a life coach
to set you on
"the right path".

There is none,

so don't make
one to go on,
but write a story that
doesn't require you
to find righteousness,
but see how unrighteous
we all are.

43. The Fires Of Hell

    Hell is a life that
is protected
toward us to
witness when we
learn about the
mountains
that are molehills
and vice versa.

    Some can tell the
difference while
most can't and
need dire help.
As for those who
don't even care
make the flames
spread all
around us.

    Let them spread faster
and more furious than
AIDS and kill more
lethally than an A-bomb
nuking this planet,
already polluted with
so many assholes,
smog, war,
famine, greed, hate,
where if we all moved
to another planet,
we'd all just do the same

thing there that we're
doing here.

Burn with the masses
or start lookin'
for matches to
create another
dust bowl,
just make it
heavenly.

44. An Event Like Any Other

There's one night
where my heart
just cannot be still
for one second,
beating erratically
with an authority
that makes the
rest of my body
vibrate with fear
and my breath leaving
my body fade into
the dark air
into the stars,
traveling
with the flies
near the trees
and the aircraft
through the clouds.

This is all
because the
weekend is
ending and
there is a
congestion of air,
along with
a week of
tasks ahead:
Wake up,
freshen up,

get dressed,
have breakfast,
go to work,
traveling with
the rest of
the world as one,
go into the day
go head first into work
while you confide with
other stiffs who
share your grief,
go home,
relax and
shake off the
mediocrity until
you put it back on
until it embeds you
to either become
ashes just before dust
or you can be buried
in the ground where
you can break bread
with the dirt.

Sunday night is a lonely moment
for all of us to endure,
reflecting on the anticipation
of the next five days where
we have a chance to do it
right and now.

It's the stomach that aches
with butterflies flapping their
wings, which make the insides

unsettling, and in addition to
my heart beating fast and
blood pumping and my mind
is set on just climbing into bed,
I'll try and forget about tomorrow,
but it's in bed waiting for lights out.

It's an event unlike any other.

45. Ill Affects Of Vitriol

I feel with a
sharpness when
I get hurt
inside after
a bad word
hits me.

I almost double over
after absorbing the
blow, shocking me
to the point of no
response, becoming
a paralysis of
my spirit, taking me
into a day of clouds,
even with the sun up.

I always wonder
why it hurts so
badly that I
may end up
crying…I hope not.

Crying is the most
horrifying thing
for a lot of us,
even before
we get to do it.

Just try to stay strong.

It's just a few words.
It's not like a knife
or a gun that'll
kill you.

There are times
where a ball of
yarn that's about to be
unveiled will expose
our feelings when
we just have to let go
of how we feel.

The tension inside
cuts itself and we melt
inside so hard,
we hurt to a point
where we might as well
show how we feel
because we, of all
people, must know
ourselves far
better than the
opposition,
even if they
know us best.

Most of all,
we must reward
them by sharing
our blood and open
our wounds to them
and drown them
with the anguish

that they've caused us.

46. Hello, I Love You

Sometimes
the best way
to meet someone
is just to say
"Hello, I love you"
because just by
the looks
you give them,
the way you can
read them from
a distance,
and by the
body language
not just the body,
it's a matter of
when you walk
over there to
tell them,
but you better
tell them,
only not
too soon.

They can see the
feelings inside of you
and read the unseen
words on your head
where you don't even
have to go over and tell
them anything.

Your outfit tells them
everything about you.
Your fortune of insecurity
without them and your
neediness to want to be
with them, and worse,
the neediness to want
to be them, among all
things, all because they
have everyone else
hungry over them.
But just go over there anyway.

47. The Road To Anomaly

Most people try
and fail to find
their own destiny,
pursuing what they
they think
it's going to be.

It turns out that whatever
it is becomes hell, realizing
their dreams start romantically
and end in tragicomedy.

Where young and optimistic
collides with old and jaded,
there are a lot of us who
know the excitement met
with the destruction of
lives accumulated with this.

This builds the masses into
an angrier herd with hope
for the ambitious looming
further overhead, elevating
into something unreachable.

It happens to
"the best of us",
is a euphemism
telling us that we're
"just not good enough"

as our dreams die,
blowing away in the wind
where the rain comes in
to pour down on our doom
to extinguish the fire stemming
from the burns and screwjobs
we've received from something
or someone or a series
of events, people, and beyond,
combined to take us into a
downward spiral, turning us from
potentially prosperous to
definitely unqualified to even
withstand even our
smallest expectations.

Where we hit the reset button,
are we really "where we need to be"
or should we just end it all in a
hurry, as long as we can find a
good hiding spot for ourselves
before we pull the trigger
or insert the syringe?

As far as we can travel to
the next life we envision
ourselves to live,
it's right around
the corner instead of
several hundred miles
or light years away.

All we have to do
is put on the brakes

and see what else
there is before we
drive towards it.

Just make it
better than
where you're at
right now.

48. Forgiveness: The Double-Edged Sword

Forgiveness is
tricky for
everyone to
undergo.

You're never
sure about
whether or not
you should just
shake hands
right after
being screwed,
sometimes for
something
you didn't do.

You're either
afraid to fight
the guilty party
or trying to fight
your demons from
the monstrosity
that you're
rightfully
about to unleash.

So, what's holding you back?
Fear,
maturity,
common sense,

peace of mind,
consequences,
or do you just
not give a damn?
Maybe you're
afraid to.
Maybe peace doesn't
allow you to worry
about it so much.
Maybe it's the
consequences
that save you.
Thing is, though
you shouldn't care
about…caring about it.

Forgiving and forgetting is
double trouble for the
multitasker trying to
make things right instead of
giving themselves the
liberty of taking liberties
on the culprit who may
force them to change
their lives with one or
two or twelve punches
with kicks, knees, stabbings,
biting and disfigurement,
resulting in an eight to
ten year timeout from
the world.

Live with the hurt until you
utter the words of exoneration

that prevents further self-vilification
and bloodlust that keeps you
thirsty for war instead of peace.

49. Shit Happens

    Sometimes taking a shit
    on the run is the only
    option that we all have,
    especially if we're out
    traveling from
    bus to bus,
    waiting room to
    waiting room,
    trying to outrun
    the shit that's
    gonna end up
    sticking in your
    underwear
    the second the
    deli cashier
    turns you down
    when you want to
    use the bathroom
    and you have no place
    else to go except
    in your pants.

    Just remember one thing…
    if you can't even go to
    the bathroom in your pants,
    you're not human.

    If you don't give a shit
    about going to the
    bathroom in your pants,

you're a brave, but
uncouth person.

You might as well die
because to live with
yourself after taking
a shit in your pants
is the ultimate power.

Shit happens, that's all!

50. Same Shit, Different Day

On some mornings,
I get scared of
waking up to
live another day
wondering
what the day will
bring to me,
only to do
the same thing
over again,
living as if
life is a
broken
record.

There may be
differences
of each day
some small
increments
of what
yesterday
brought,
otherwise
I'm going
through
motions
flowing
in the air
just so I can

get from
point A to
point B, C, D
all the way down
to Z.

So why am I scared
to wake up for
before each day
begins?

Do I worry
myself about
whether or not
I'm gonna come out
the other side with
that sigh of relief
that I did
only to do
it all over
again?

The nervousness
that I have is stage
fright that
festers inside
me before I
wake up to
perform each day
of the week
on a grand stage,
round or flat,
that I'm playing
a role that I

want to see
how badly I want
redundancy to end.

Same shit,
different day,
even more chilling
feelings.

51. My Heart: The Largest Muscle In My Body

My heart is
a muscle that is
stronger as
it is weaker,
where I use it to fight,
win or lose.

When I win,
it beats louder
than a drum,
but when I lose,
it absorbs the
harm that's
so intense that
I breathe extra
heavily to
withstand the
trauma
and lean on
the walls to
remain upright
only to stagger
with a great passion.

Sometimes
I don't know
if I want to
win or lose
as I live and die
by a sword of feelings

so sharp that its
intensity makes me
dizzy and lethargic
with heavy limbs
and distorted
equilibrium,
dying gracefully
with each strong
emotion.

52. Free In My Cocoon

I've always felt
inhibited, slow,
and muzzled
by the weight of my
own tension.
It's a big, hard, iron muscle
and it has me moving slower
than when I start to
turn old, which is when I
can start doing that,
like I'm being trapped
in quicksand,
only going through air,
wondering how fast
or slow I'm movin'.

Don't matter where
I'm at or who I'm with,
the world I'm in and
the life I live is
feelin' far slower
and stronger
than just livin'
uncomfortably
by way of
just feeling
funny.

I can't seem to
enjoy the

enjoying that
life has hidden
from me when
I move around
to find the joy
outside me
in a place
where I can
only fit so
little time
to smile,
eat my favorite food,
listen to my
favorite music,
frolic in my
cocoon before
I tense up and
face the days
that will kill
me from
hypertension
when YOU least
expect it.

53. Going Boldly Where I Never Want To Go Again

Sometimes,
I get scared
of the dark side
I always trap
inside of me
not wanting to
rage out as it
hurts me to feel
ugly,
making me
want to puke
where exactly
this means
vomiting
the darkness
festering
inside of me,
knowing that
darkness itself
will become blacker
than a psychopath's
coffee the more
it's hidden and
hiding creates more
of a stir to want to
kill you more deeply.

Sometimes, I envision the
consequences that if I do
indeed kill, I picture

myself running away
from the cops the second
I commit the crime.

I don't want to see myself
getting chased by cops
and then arrested before
ending up in prison,
where I would be bullied,
beaten, abused, raped,
miserable, and then killed.
I don't want one mood swing
to cost me my freedom,
but I know anger can help me
feel and give me a rush,
taking me to a place
I've never been before.

I just hope it's not jail.

54. Arise From The Compost Of Hurt

A scarcity of
pain threshold
has liberated a legion
of worn down,
overworked,
disenfranchised stiffs
around the world
only giving them more
firepower to stave off
uncomfortability
and a repression
that paralyzes a
universe where
even the brightest
lights become dim
with no voice to
callout the pain
while laying in it.

If you're hurt,
say it,
show it,
live it,
embrace it,
but don't bury it…
In fact, don't get buried in it.

55. Bird's Eye View Of A Dystopia

These are times
where I wish I
can fly in the sky
and see all the
air traffic around me,
but most at all,
I want to see all
of the activity that
is being performed in
this soulful, yet soulless world,
all while it's being soulful.

I'll have a
bird's eye view
of books being robbed,
bar fights breaking out,
teenage douchebags drag racing
in the wee hours of the morning
in their parents' car,
bonfires on top of
convenience stores,
bombs going off on
mountain tops,
rabid dogs chasing
little boys up the street.

More importantly,
will I see more of
those things instead of
seeing people sharing

or helping others in need,
besides in need of
expressing feelings
of hate, anger, malice,
or anything that will
diminish our Earth
further that it's been?

Maybe if those problems
go away, humanity does
because acting out is
part of being human.
If we don't act out,
we don't really live,
but if we do,
the tightness inside
all of us agonizes
our will to feel peace.

Then again, maybe that's what
we need anyway.

Which is more liberating and fun?!?

56. Conscious While Unconscious

The hardest thing to do
is wake up in the
morning, especially
when you anticipate
each waking...or
sleeping hour,
wondering what time
it is and how much
more sleep you have
until you crawl
out of bed just to
wake yourself up.

You may be awake
just to move around,
but the world's a blur
and there's no bliss
to embrace.

The cobwebs and daydreams
run around in my head
just to make me feel
all shuttery while all
I want is a hot shower
to wash away the insanity.

Problem is, though,
the sanity I gain from the
shower conforms me into a
well-functioning statistic

of disgruntlement.

If we can remain insane
throughout our lives and
maybe hide the sanity
and inject more of the livid
in us all, we can all probably
become better members of
society, where everyone can
be more than welcome to
see the Hyde, yet we'd somehow
have to hide the Jekyll instead.

Otherwise, the tension keeps
us at bay and makes us more
unreachable with who we are
and who we need to be.

Where that becomes the game
within the game, it also becomes
a blur whether your waking up
or fully alert to everything
except yourself, most of all.

57. Youth Fades

A bad back that
hurt for about seven
years is like a life scar
that no one can see,
but only you can feel,
where moving any way
you want takes away
the youth and versatility
you want back to
give yourself the life
you didn't live, all because
you did what you wanted.

Living then vs. living now
makes you think about
which life is already
better than the other.

The answers are hidden,
but overall, it's something
where you have to pick
and choose each day…
live in the past or
preserve your future?

Everybody's
a detective,
trying to figure out
other people's problems,
but live in a maze

Anathematic Darkness

trying to solve their
own, living in their own heads
wondering what's
happening there as well
as in their own lives.

And this all started
with a bad back…
Jesus…I guess
it can start with that
or a hangnail or a
full moon…whatever.

Where have all the days
of my youth gone so quickly?

They left me considering
who I need to be now that
I'm older, wiser, maybe,
but missing in a maze,
looking for a meaning,
only to go around in circles.

58. Russian Roulette

There are many days
where I can kill
for a natural breeze
outside, especially after
walking through the
humidity, swimming
in dry sweat and
writhe at, wondering where
the latest bar is that is, at least
a moderately strong fan
to turn my sweaty body
into a snow cone.

Sometimes, I'm just
waiting for my stomach
to stop aching from
starvation, others,
to stop aching from
being filled up of
so much junk the road
has to offer where
only survival
is shown through
eating whatever
you can to hold you over
filling a hole in your gut
when you're not
gaining any caloric value,
but finding a means to survive.

Sometimes, though,
surviving is not even
touchin' your money
to spend on a pizza or a Coke…
Thing is…
you choose when you
wanna starve…
Now or later
when you're 70 and you've
outlived your means?

What's it matter?
Death is waiting for you
to give out and end up…
dead.

Dead with your eyes
rolled over your head,
not knowing that
no matter what you choose,
it's a game of
Russian roulette.

59. Breaking News

It's only a matter of time
until an unexpressed feeling
becomes a breaking news story.

What type of newscast
are we gonna watch
this time?

A mass murder in the hallway
of a local high school,
all within the squeezing
of the trigger of a Glock
or the raging temper of
a suit in a big skyscraper
who just ate his last insult,
or a repressed cabbie,
who honks his horn
after being cut off
for the thousandth time
by a dude haulin' a Tesla.

It can leak out your neck,
you can rip if off your chest,
or you can indirectly displace
their feelings reserved for
that special someone
to someone who's never
seen the likes of you
before in their life.

Anathematic Darkness

Whatever the mood is,
it looks real bad,
but it feels so good…
until you get older and
sick and tired of having
these emotions…
tightness starts to creep
upon you and put you
through a workout
that'll make Marines
bootcamp look like a
siesta in Cancun.

Take out the trash and
empty out your soul,
because when the Sanitation
comes in the mornin' and
your garbage ain't sittin'
in front of your house,
they're gonna drive off
and you're gonna be stuck
with the stench, the smell,
and the weight of your own
baggage and deep-seated angst.

60. The Death Of Dystopia Depends On The People Who Build One

The life we choose may
be determined for us
as a metaphysical system
has insolent options
that we must take to
decide our own fate
when we're worthy of
having more as a
worldwide union.

A better living is not
just on all of us, but
those who share what
they want to keep,
most of all, what they don't need.

The death of dystopia
depends on the people
who build one.

That's how unexpressed feelings
turn a world into a volcano
erupting one riot at a time.

Yes, some people may die,
but worldview evaporates
when variety of living,
chain free isn't
acknowledged,

let alone, embraced.

61. What Do You Want To Be When You Pass On?

When you're called
to pass on,
you won't want to
anyway.

Mysteriously, though we die
when we are called
upon, only it's our
spirit that hears the call
instead of us.

We're waiting and
wondering when
our time comes
or we're just living
moment to moment
chasing the demons
away from taking us
without even noticing.

Nobody wants to wake up
with a list of things to do
just like nobody wants to
read a list of things to do.

It's a dogmatic list of chores
to do when all you want to do
is listen to your spirit and have it
guide you, even when it tells you
it's time to perish and go.

Hearing the soothing voice tell
us our time is now to decease
and pass to another world where
only spirits are aloud and solid
flesh and blood are prohibited
from discovery of a transcendent
universe, only they can either
become feast of the maggots
or transform into ashes.

No one wants to die,
but you need to ask yourself:
What do I want to be after
I die? Do I want to become
food in the ground or dust
floating in the wind?

62. Being And Doing

A human being
is someone who is,
who was is now and
who will become
forevermore.

A human doing
is someone
who does,
is doing,
and who did,
only to do again.

Can we be both
or do we
have to choose?

Or...
are we allowed
to be both?

Would it benefit to be both?

Are we both actually?

Do we have to be one
or the other?

What if a human being
doesn't become and

what do they become by
not becoming?

Depending on what they
don't become makes
them become a failure,
but is there a negative
connotation to it?

Same with a human doing,
if you don't do, what have you done?

Whatever existence we have
for the time in which we live,
we think so much about what
we want to do and what we
have to do.

We think about what we
don't want to do where
what we choose is who
we become, even if
we don't expect to,
even when we don't
see it coming?

63. Resetting The Table

Waiting to discover
this land we live on
is wandering around
a world that's
filled with lost souls,
thinking they gave an answer
to everything about
how they're high rollin',
livin' "the good life" when
it's right under
their nose that they
aren't, not knowing
that the people who
want to live like the
elites are doing better
than they think, even
after a natural disaster
named disappointment
wiped away their hopes
and dreams with the wind.

If this is you, let those
hopes of the past stay there
and use your intuition
to pry open a new world,
create it, but don't tell anyone
except where you've
been.

Break out the brick and mortar

and this time, build a bigger wall,
but this time, add steel and turn
yourself into a fortress for the
marketplace to try and throw
the hardest stone or build
the biggest bomb in front
of you to see what happens
this time around.

There's no enemy like the
past, but there's no better
feeling than upgrading into
a secretary of defense to go
with the tornado of talent
being possessed.

These are the weapons and
shields of battle that give
us the strength to withstand
humanity and mankind
for generations to come.

64. My Brain Works, But My Mind Doesn't

Lunch time is a time
where my spirit
is sagging and I'm choking
on my own phlegm,
anticipating the taste of
my tuna fish sandwiches
when all I really need is
to sit down and breathe.

Sometimes, it's not even about
sitting down to eat or recharge
my batteries.

It becomes more and more
about trying to search through
the clouds in my head and
getting through to the inside
to see what's going on while
I'm in a mad dash to refuel,
knowing that I'm still
gonna linger with fatigue.

My hunger pains aren't from
lack of replenishment, but
from the blankness that my
mind suffers for a 30 minute
span, wondering what my mind
is thinking about through the
subconscious and how do I
find it.

I'm so lost in the clouds,
I can't even hear my heart beat.

I know one thing – when I'm in
the clouds searching for a way
out of the middle of nowhere
so I can think, I can't even.

I'm so worn out that I can't
even imagine myself sitting
down to eat while doing so,
my mind is such a black hole,
even though my brain gives
messages to my body to
sit down and eat.

I can't even daydream about
flying through the sky where
I can direct the wind to follow
me into every continent I
travel into.

65. The Fear Of Having Fear

Just because I'm
grown up doesn't
mean that I'm
not afraid of
anything because
I'm more afraid
of who I may become.

Old is one thing
because it's
different from young.

Sometimes it
goes hand in hand
with being jaded,
where we may have
lived through the
worst years…
except they may
live through us with
our feelings, along with
our thoughts and then our actions,
which come hand in hand
with those feelings,
which then creates them.
Maybe it's time
to find something
blissful to do,
like grow flowers,
dance like La Parka,

or eat healthier,
or…

Forget about
money and
tryin' to live.
Forget about tryin'!

Forget!

Fear makes you forget about
where you are, who you are,
and the fact that you're alive
where your stream of
consciousness comes to a
streaking halt.

The fact that we all come
in contact with fear can
make us feel worthless,
having that feeling control
everything inside and outside
of us, having a feeling of
helplessness.

The fear of having fear,
in a nutshell.

66. Soft Isn't Always Strong

I can't decide
if my heart is either
strong or weak.

I use it to
bathe through
every day
while stressed out
while others use it
to get what they want
from me without
even knowing.

Battling these
obstacles as a
routine to survive begins
to wear me out where
I can't keep up
sometimes where too many
beats will wear me down.

Maybe it's both, so you'll
have to take the good
with the bad because
we can't always
save the world.

Even Superman had
to take a siesta and
as for Batman?

Anathematic Darkness

Last time I checked,
he moved out of
Gotham because
the crime rate and
law enforcement
were so equally horrible
that he split!

Remember when the Joker
got away after causing
so much chaos in The Dark Knight?

Yeah, man…that's was rough.

Sometimes patience is
what builds the heart,
but impatience gives
the heart room to beat
as hard and as loud
as it needs to.

You're gonna suffer,
but how much
more painless
can you make it?

The more painless you make it,
the stronger your heart has to be.

Whether you think lovely thoughts,
ignore your prosecutors, refrain
from revenge, don't waste time
regretting, or turn the other cheek,

you'll still bleed from the inside out,
even if you mean well because the
other person doesn't so much.

Soft can be strong, but
isn't always.

67. Comfort

We are one,
big, wide,
king-sized town with
such a homely, suburban
feel that I feel like
I'm in a neverending city.

You got your Dairy Queens,
your little barnyards,
suburbs, your rural communities,
where people mask their
evil and dress up to be
as wholesome as they can be,
hiding the cynicism
from the kids and
from the neighbors,
while patrons can
scope out a sliver
of that darkness
by seeing their body language
break down the tension
they have where they share
a sweet rage that the kids
won't see until they're all alone
without any witnesses.

Otherwise,
when I look around
and I see small shops,
houses lined up together,

regular everyday people,
I see a reality,
which is a mediocrity
that we all try to
wrestle out of it
only for the rest of
society to wrestle
them into it just by
telling them what
not to do while
they're doing
the same thing.

There's a whole universe
of mediocrity that people
consider as excellence,
only we never seem to
see through the goodness,
but into the goodness,
thinking everything is going
to be okay instead of piercing
through the pain of its goodness
to see what exactly makes it so
when we want the doom to
drip through its cracks and
seduce us into anarchical
madness, which is justice
barging into the wholesomeness
and melting the facade of
the utopia we retain through
fear of our own potential.

68. Heatwave

The heatwave we live in
puts us in a bubble,
where all we can do is live in sweat,
hot air, and burning exhaustion.

This bubble suffocates us all
by having us live through this,
breathing in heat and exhaling it,
while sweating in this hell,
where it becomes a
lifestyle, melting us into
water, spreading this heat
wherever we go and wherever
we look to escape to.

This is a season where we can
turn our mushy hearts into
demonic ones walking down
the streets, shootin' hoops
in the playground, and if you're
homeless, draggin' your
mattress into the shade
only to live in humidity.

Swimming in perspiration
makes me feel like I'm drowning
in my jeans while the life
I'm in is nothing more than
a sweatshop with burning air
that turns you into a world

of warm liquid.

That the only type of swimming
most people can afford to do
if they can't afford to install
a pool in their backyard,
so they drown in sweat and
walk through the hot air
slowly from the sun beating
down on them, forcing us to
gasp, doubling over in
exhaustion, awaiting a
heat stroke to end this struggle.

Owned by the sun,
it's only a matter of time
before this I
descend into water.

69. Rambunctious Feelings

Rambunctious feelings
of panic puncture me
like a sharp pick through
my intestines.

Waking up,
tossing and turning,
looking for comfort
by breathing,
by living,
by dumping
my pain in the air
to air out the holes
in my stomach
while the blood
flies out of my mouth
into our world,
representing
the inner conflict
that makes us
bleed deep inside
or just form a
ball of hate.

Self loathing keeps us
all awake where we do
nothing more than think
about how no one likes us,
how we can't do certain things,
how we feel about ourselves –

we sleep on our pain and we
dive into mental debauchery
as we meditate on our
self loathing.

The more we feel the burn,
the more we toss and turn,
breathe heavily, burst into
tears and hide our faces
into the pillow, praying
no one sees us like this.

You can be hurt in
any way possible,
only you don't choose it,
nor can you predict it,
but it's a ball of hurt
in its own right.

Its rambunctiousness festers
and travels inside my intestines,
and it haunts my spirit to inject
intimidation into my being,
forcing me to shake and
shiver, becoming the puppet
master, controlling me to
bite my nails, hold myself
and shiver in fear.

If only I can take a deep breath
and count to ten, one digit
at a time, I can slowly bring back
the courage I once had to become
the fearless human being I've

always dreamed of, where the
strings attached to my back
come off and the power
accumulates to give me
the calm to be free again.

70. The Repression We Carry

The emotion of anger
has strings attached
to my back
where it controls my
every move,
filled with a toxicity
of hurt aggravating me
as I feel a heavy black bag
of garbage bring down my soul
because I'm in a bad mood.

It's baggage, all right,
but I carry it like a
banker carrying his briefcase
with an ease that people
don't even notice,
all because I'm trying to
hold everything together
so I don't become another
statistic where another madman
comes to work picking off people
one at a time.

That's the rest of us with
the repression we carry,
waiting for someone
tender enough to
take it out on,
someone more poor
than us.

Someone more weird
than us,
someone more understanding
than us,
someone weaker
than us,
and by that, I mean
stronger,
in fact so strong as
to endure the pain
we pass on
from us to them,
where they'll eventually
do the same,
only of having
that prickly high
dominating our
subordinates
of society,
but most of all,
our moral fiber.

71. Stuntman's High

Eustress is a higher level
of pain threshold where
I want to experience
each day for the rest
of my life.

I want to ride a race car
400 mph into a gasoline truck,
explode and come back for more.

I want to jump off the
Empire State Building onto
a giant stack of flaming
tables and land onto
mattresses with explosives
wrapped onto it and scorpions
crawling in a water tank.

I want to fly in the sky
at warp speed and crash
through Mount Everest
and out through Mount Fuji,
hook a right and float into
outer space.

I want to jump so high
trying to slam dunk that
I take off into the sky,
disrupting someone's flight
to Athens and redirect it to

the Moon before I come
down and monster dunk
the ball and shatter the
backboard, sharing a
piece of glass with
all of my fans in
attendance to witness.

Watching me throw down
wins you a free glass fragment
to take home with you.

I want work as if I'm
riding the Cyclone at
Astroland Theme Park,
riding wildly while doing
the most mundane thing of all…
sitting at home watching paint dry.

Most of all, I want to
rest peacefully without
interruption after going
on those adventures to
reflect on the journeys,
only to dream about new
ones to embark on.

That's much cooler than
wanting to be the President
of the US or a billionaire.

72. R&R Should Be The Devil's Workshop

If you don't yawn
at least once in your life,
you've never been tired…
and you need to recharge.

It's healthy to be
fatigued, tuckered out,
and screaming to go
upstairs with a yawn.

It's just that when
you yawn too loud,
day or night,
at home or at work,
it's time to go to bed.

If you're at home,
go up to bed,
but if you're still at work
and you're yawning so loud
that your boss can hear it
from their office on the
top floor of that skyscraper
you work at in the city,
punch out now so
your mind can escape
to paradise while
your body melts
under the sun while
laying on the sand.

Go to bed and become
one with your bed sheets
and mattress, sinking
further into the fabric and
live peacefully as you sleep
deeply into the serene.

It's when you go to sleep,
the phone rings or someone
decided to come visit you
or someone stalks you to
validate their madness
by stealing your calm.

Peace is something we all
chase, but war is something that
chases us more vehemently.

Which one will we be able
to reach us first?

73. The Social Maze

People are a big maze
to have to walk through
just to realize that
you can live
however you want,
except you won't know
how to, just as they
walk through you.

People are the ultimate
obstacle course,
where we have to
find a way around
and vice versa.

You and them are
feuding each day
where sometimes
after "Good morning",
the games begin
while sometimes,
they start even
before you two
even meet.

Difference of opinion
in favorite ice cream
can start a fight,
let alone why you
should get a raise

or play Hamlet,
yet root for the Yankees.

Trying to understand them
hands on is an abnormal psychology
class with additional
social sciences included.

As for humanities,
that's a mystery because
it's hard to find that
anywhere.

And even if you have
advanced degrees in it,
sometimes the streets can't
even prepare you for
the abstract life you're
about to live.

74. Start Living Or Keep Dying

Wondering can be too much
because sometimes
there's nothing else to do,
thanks to just simple
layin' back,
droppin' your guard,
letting the world live
so you can do the same
is the rocket fuel
that's behind the wondering.

Sittin' alone on your bed
while the radio's on,
but your curiosity
and wildest dreams are
louder than anything
you'll listen to at
the highest volume
goes to show that
you're already dreaming
of a better world
that only you want to
create and make everyone
around you
surrender to it.

That's a thought coming
from not getting any
or enough attention
or mapping out a plan

to take over the world
where only you can hear
you own world blast off
while the world you live in
has become a blasted,
beaten down universe,
flooded with problems
that either get
better or worse.

While you're dreaming
and even if you start doing,
it's gonna get worse…
and better.

Problem is your world
will be worse if you
don't change it while
it's getting better…
or maybe it's better
while you're getting
worse

Find a fellow misanthrope
to wallow to, and dream
together on how you think
you can change what you
can't even control,
or sometimes,
even see.

Dance furiously into
fire, moonwalk onto
the sun, do an Irish jig

on tightropes, and breakdance
into the sky together,
but most of all, rest in peace,
knowing you did all those
things and enjoyed each
second of cementing
your legacy as an oddity,
but a talented one at that.

75. Unkemptness = Control

To be unkempt
is to be a force
to shatter the earth
like glass and shake
it to its core like a
pair of maracas,
whether it's through
behavior, disposition,
skill level, plan of action,
or just plain on a mission
to live on your terms…
That's unkempt because
it's supposed to be
exploring a world that
you haven't examined
that otherwise, examines,
eats up, spits out or
swallows whole,
depending on the mood
it's in and internalizes
your tenderness
to make itself stranger
with it.

That's when you stop
pretending, caring,
worrying, thinking,
or living,
where all you
can do is shut

out the universe
and have nothing
control you,
just don't try to
control anything
either.

Let everything go on
automatic by itself,
on its own,
step back and
watch it go.

Look out the window
and watch the
hurricane,
train wreck,
and volcano
unravel so much
with a weight
attached to it
that you can use
an earthquake strong enough
to try for a utopia…
yeah, good luck.

76. Feast Or Famine

Drenched in their own sweat,
swimming from town to town
when they're really walking
or running or trying to make it
from place to place,
so they can discover what
this land will offer
people of other worlds,
while depriving their own
citizens of minority.

I can't always lend
a dollar to the needy,
but I can sympathize
what it's like to be shut out,
unwanted, or less needed
than the others who have
their friends wanting them
so they can play with
their pricks and ruin the world
while people who are needed
are drowning in perspiration
wanting to be needed,
auditioning to matter
in a planet, round or flat,
where we need the
smallest people who
have the strongest hearts,
minds, and souls to
build a world,

where all can lead and
live in based on love
for the lesser
and keep a watchful
eye on the overpaid.

Each day is an audition
to see if you can live
through struggle and
random days of hunger
to win the role of being
the lucky one to not
have to go through that
anymore.

We're all hungry for something,
driven to a certain degree, but
it takes someone who is set
ablaze to run through the
others to eat the most and
the most often.

77. Death Comes With Life

Time flies when you're
havin' fun,
but it moves too slow
when you're not.

Either way,
we're gonna get through
the day closer to our
final resting place.

Each second passing by,
we're dying just as we're
living to be who we want to,
only we dream of our future,
not fully grasping the fact
that the world will no longer
need us while our families
will miss us and remember
what we've done for them.

We live to create our mark,
then make it, no matter what
it is, we live to breathe air
into our congested generation
and with each droplet, it becomes
a rainbow, as each color changes
the face of the Earth in each generation
we all contribute to, which is
what makes this world go
round and round to keep

our universe productive
for mankind to keep
preserving what we have
left behind.

78. Nobody's Perfect, But Complete

Everybody has wants
and needs, chippin' away
to realize their own
self-actualization,
only to understand
that at the end,
all we need to know
is that we want more,
whether you need,
want, what you want,
and what you can't live without.

Not having things that
we can't live without
maximizes our needs
while it minimizes
our wants.

We may have money,
but don't have class,
have class,
but no brains,
brains,
but no friends,
friends,
but no lovers,
lovers,
but no family,
family,
but no place to live.

Nobody is ever complete,
but this, in itself, makes us
perfect in who we are,
and nothing is.

So if we're not
perfect,
we might be,
somehow complete.

79. Outta Love, Outta Sight, Outta Mind

There isn't any more love
to go around because
she won't give me any
and I ran out of love to give
after I used it up on her,
someone that didn't care
that I existed.

Putting all your eggs
in one basket's
gonna cause it to
explode with the
eggs cracking
into a puddle of yolks,
waiting for some unlucky
gal to slip and fall into
a world of unlimited texts,
unanswered calls and
unrelenting desperation.

Hey, I haven't seen you in a while.
Whatcha doin' this weekend?

Hey there, what's up? Did I wake you?

Hey, are you home?

Yeah, I'd block me too.

God, man…

Why doesn't someone
try pickin' me up
where I can learn
sumthin' new?

Just don't make the same
mistakes that I made.

80. Journey Of A Swollen Heart

Hearts swell up when
they feel love,
but pop like a balloon
when they feel pain.

It's like blowing up
a tube float in your pool
when someone tells you
how cute you are,
the heart blows up,
and hovers inside
your body.

When a heart breaks,
it shrivels like a prune,
making one double over
in pain.

Hearts are tender,
which is a euphemism
for the vulnerable,
but when it's built up,
it will last for eternity
before it grows with age
becoming a matter of time
before it gives out.

When it breaks,
your soul bleeds,
so, you have to wait

for it to bleed out
before you're even
ready to heal,
breathe, cry, and
let you mind
go to hell and
then stay there.

Then dig your way out,
as long as you climb back
into contention of the world
and play the music better
than when you face it.

81. Dreams And Nightmares

I live in two worlds:

One,
where I see, hear and
witness everything in front
of me, able to touch things,
feel things,
and experience them.

Another,
where I see,
hear, and witness
everything
in front of me,
only they touch me,
feel me,
and thrill me.

There's an ebb and flow
I experience when I undergo
the travel through these
world's in order for me to
touch and to be touched.

This is a reciprocating
tide taking you in to
see where you'll end up…
living the dream of
witnessing the ocean and
all of its beautiful glory

or being sucked in by the
current and eventually
drown in the middle of it all.

Sometimes,
I can't experience
my dreams,
but I sure can
experience
my nightmares.

82. Fear Looking For A Friend

Lovingly,
I talk myself
into a happy mood
when I'm scared to death,
only to realize that
the same things happen
every day.

That's when the fear
goes away.

That's when it should
come right back.

Thing is,
I've become numb
to routine,
but I can still
go out and play at night,
so maybe this life
will talk to me
lovingly in return,
to turn me in to
a local boob that
can still be a child…
spiritually.

I can still go out and play
in the night, washing
away my stressors until

my head hits the pillow
in unison with the moon
and the stars, where I can rest
the demons until I wake
the next day to tame them,
preventing fear from being
injected into my system.

All it wants to do is engage
with me to do its best to
arouse my soul for the better
and wake me up while I
want to live more happily
without its need to enlighten
me to be afraid and cope with it.

Enough days of fear, instead,
go ahead and fear me.

83. My Last Week Of Summer In Elkton

Before we fall into autumn,
summer sticks around
to melt my love handles
and turn me into a puddle
of perspiration.

Walking into the strips of
East Pulaski Highway
made me think of
several things:

How perseverant the sun is,
as it continues to shine
to melt my worries while
I walk around just to
discover instead of
getting some citrus and exercise.

Also, that evolution is
just a Google search away.

I'm just looking for another
place to explore next.

Also, I live the life of the seeker,
where my loneliness gives me
the green light to be the
vagabond needed to survive
my own existence,
working the weekdays,

traveling the weekends,
bussing, cabbing,
roaming the land that wants
to eat us up when we're
hopeless.

When we're hapless, though,
the road morphs us into concrete,
where they say,
"The road becomes my bride."

Instead, we'll become
the road's bitch,
with everywhere to go,
but not knowing where.

Wandering is probably the
best way to travel for me
so I don't have to have an
itinerary to go by except
go from one place to
another and then back.

Then we sit around and
wait for the leaves to fall,
looking for a cool breeze
to compliment the
upcoming season.

84. Spoken Words of Wonder

Some people live as if there's
nothing's wrong with anything
in a world where everything is
happening at once, good or bad,
right and wrong, no matter what.

It's like we're living in a place
where we search for a meaning.

I feel like I'm squatting in a world
that defies the wanderers,
not because they wonder,
but they won't conform
in order to wander.

No purpose or place, but
taking each day as it comes
without creating anything.

There's a ton of smoke
around most of us who
can't quite find a rhythm
on where to go and what to do.

As for the people we drive by
and ride with are stuck,
living in psychological ruin,
joining the herd army
to hunt down those
who've found their way

to support the cause
of the rich getting richer.

Only this herd are unearthed
with vision and curiosity,
just no one to reach out to
and care for, but most people
care for themselves and
bitterly reject assistance,
feeling stronger to go it alone.

People who live alone and
push away from convention
are the poorest, but bravest
of them all, living without
approval, only if they were
striving for something
more ambitious, I can see
them all scurrying for help
and assurance.

Thing is, assurance comes
to haunt us where it tells us
things are great, but greatness
must be upheld consistently
and that's almost impossible.

Everyone wants to be safe
and have acceptance, only
to realize that being denied
is part of that path, which
makes people not want any
part of society, because
they're scared of being

denied, but most of all,
stuck with acceptance of
being a part of something that
keeps them around, but doesn't
love them enough they way
they need to be.

85. Five Finger Discount Of Utopia

Walking in a deafening
sound of silences at
Ryan Homes in an eerie,
yet utopian land in Elkton
scared me to wonder if
anyone in the state of
Maryland even knew
this neighborhood
existed.

Ridgley Forest embodies
Pleasantville,
Levittown,
Orange County,
and just about
every world that scares me
worse than the slums
ever will.

Suburban banality
is an underworld,
where the masses
lick their chops
at that pretty house,
only to live with
their allies,
especially
who never forgot
the struggle,
to bond with the
underlings about

how poor we are,
but can't leave the
dilapidated life.

I understand some people
want to live more peacefully
enjoying that same deafening
sound of silence and embrace
serenity, but sometimes,
that could be a sign for
intruders to see the unseen
target in every neighborhood,
telling them to come in and
take everything you need.

Serenity is the white noise
that screams out for burglars
to be the Robin Hood of their
own life, where if you can't
afford the life you want,
you best come take it,
any way you can.

86. Ramble Poem About Liberation

How does anyone
know how to endure
what they're
paid to?

How do they
endure what they're
paid to do?

Sometimes,
it's luck that bails
them out of
a jam of a day.

Piles of mail
to deliver,
listening to an
asshole scream,
or flip so many
burgers that
your wrists get
sprained.

Auditioning
twenty-five hundred
actors for the next
big Hollywood blockbuster
or eating cat shit to
become a reality TV dad
for a few grand.

What did you do
with that money?

Cop a few bags of
dope and scrape enough
change to go to
rehab?

Hey, ya gotta
keep workin'!

I know what it's like to
do something I don't
wanna do.

The gridlock involved where
there's no place to go
becomes a dark place
where you're in a
traffic jam and you wanna
jump out of the car and
walk the rest of the way
to your destination,
only to add more jam
to the traffic all sandwiched
together where no one can move.

That goes to show that
you're thinking about
other people when you
need to think about
just getting out.

Anathematic Darkness

Give yourself the VIP
treatment and leave the rest
in the street and let them wait
for someone to move it.

Abandon the rest of the pack
and make yourself peerless
to boldly live in ways you
never lived before.

87. Either/Or

My mind always tells me
that I can do it,
but reality shows that
I can't quite yet.

Even when I do it
right, wrong, or
my way,
it's still not enough.

In my mind, it's the best
thing I've ever seen,
but when I do it,
it's the worst thing
that we've all ever seen.

Where is the in-between
because the best is yet
to come, mainly because
I'm still working on it
while people say it's
either/or.

I may never find what's
considered the best, worst,
or the in-between,
but I keep doing it
anyway even if the
nothingness comes out
in the end because I
I have to see it,

even if I can't.

I wonder a lot about how
I want to be seen when
doing something because
image is a big thing,
even for those who are the
least polarizing figures,
even in their own home.

Sometimes, I see myself
as cool enough, or I might
not be nearly as cool as I
want to be, but what's even
better is that I don't want to
have the job of needing to
be cool. People who have that
problem may not have to
work as hard as others.

88. Hunger And Will Meets Solace

Sometimes my hunger
and will overload and I feel like
I can take on the galaxy
and everything is gonna
be fine, except things
aren't and they're
getting worse than
they should be.

My heart… or is it my soul which
gets antsy and it's exciting
because I'm actually happy…?

It's just that one moment
that I have where happiness
comes and goes.

How long is this going to last?

It feels good to have
these feelings while I'm
eating my breakfast,
or riding the bus, enjoying
the simple things like sitting
in the back seat of the bus
while I enjoy my breakfast,
feeling that this should last forever.

Sometimes, it will last
for a little while longer

than it should, longer
than it would, or
longer than you actually want
but when it ends, let's put it
this way…

Every sentence comes to an end…

Where only the sentence
of happiness is something
that most are imprisoned for life
with, not seeing the ignorance
of their ways, making them
feel even happier and less
likely to care about the
cons that life has for us.

When people live a sentence
of doom, they look for a way
out by searching for the truth
of the issue without walking
away from the problem.

Finding solace in this essence
is essential.

89. Separating Man From Animal

My temper scares me
more than it scares you.

I revolt angrily in order
to fight off the demons
that you cast upon me
so I can keep myself
safe and you even safer,
otherwise, my growing frustration is
giving me a panic attack
so you better have one
before I give you a
broken skull and a
heart attack.

I'll be angrier than I
can afford to be,
especially now that
I'm older and more afraid
and with that, even more courageous,
where it's a life that I don't even
want to waste yelling at you.

Please, please…
stay away from me
as this interaction is
starting to scare me.

Don't make me want to hurt
you, or even myself from

hurting you, as it scares me
so from causing evil, but
keeps me in check from
unleashing the animal,
keeping it at bay from the
other humans.

90. In The Waiting Room For Death

Wandering my mind away
about being depressed has
become a big internal
issue for me.

Sometimes I wonder how
others feel inside about
themselves and their
current lives.

Sometimes, I wonder how
I even feel about my
own life, as I live with
constant thoughts about
when I'm going to die.

I'm at the halfway point
where I will ask myself,
"When will I perish?"

I'm knocking on death's door,
asking the Reaper when he'll
come to pick me up where
he says, "I'll let you know
when I knock on your door."

I guess when my number's up,
Death'll let me know, but it's
something of a conversation
that I want to discuss with

him about what death is like.

Tell me everything that I
Should know about what
to expect.

I'm predicting that I'll drop
dead in my sleep on a Sunday
afternoon while dozing off
on my living room recliner
at home all on my own.

Either hunched over, head
down with my mouth open
or laid out and reclined on
the chair.

If I had to choose when to
go or when I'm ready to die,
I would say to Death,
"When I'm in so much pain,
I can't even move or
I'm all out of money
where I can't make
any more I'm in so
much pain."

But what exactly is
Death?

Is it literally dying or
is it me being broke and poor?

91. Decades Of Anathematic Darkness

Willing to go the extra mile
overall in my life, we punish
ourselves, working in shambles
to become something that
only a handful of us are
lucky to become…
recognized in a world,
whether in the streets,
on social media,
or even in our own homes,
we don't even have the time
or the place to stick our heads
out and discuss our day at work,
on the road, out in an irrational
universe, but so much has
happened where we are
unwilling to explain that we
express it indirectly and
painfully irascible.

As I'm stuck in a world
between showcasing shame
and reserving it for the
right people to feel I do
so only they can live the
ruptures of their souls
enough to compare
themselves to me.

When they look in the

mirror the next time
they wake up with my
struggles stuck in their mind
in the middle of the night,
they'll see how I feel,
how my friend wrestled
me to the ground face
first on the floor in
front of his TV set in
his bedroom while
playing NBA Showdown
on Super Nintendo,
grinding away at me.

They'll see how I feel
when I got brutally
beaten while pinned to
the fence on the
playgrounds, breaking out
in fear, in tears, and a
timeline of hurt and deep
sadness that include rumbling
nerves that come ahead.

They'll see the anxieties ahead
that will one day lead to my future
fears and compounded years of
heartbreak formed into a
capacity crowd of millions just
staring, waiting for me to react
with weakness.

People are not worth going the
extra mile for when all they

want to do is damage on you.

As a child, your schoolmates
in the playground help build
your threshold while your
parents help you sustain it.

Bad customers play a factor
in keeping it hardened,
so why do we all cry so much
then?

Some can melt down these
walls with each tear we
exit out from underneath us.

To build the strength
of our souls where it
will help break down
the walls, which separate
us from the torn heartstrings,
waiting to be tied back
together again.

About the Author

Tom Cintula is an independent author and writer who was born, raised and currently resides in Staten Island, New York. He is a graduate of The College of Staten Island with dual bachelor's degrees in Sociology/Anthropology and Philosophy. His previous publishing efforts include poetry collections such as *Sonnetsphere* and *Sirius*. His previous writing credits include contributions for *The Borgen Project*, *Game 7 Sports Club*, and *All Access MMA*.

www.ingramcontent.com/pod-product-compliance
Lightning Source LLC
Chambersburg PA
CBHW050311010526
44107CB00055B/2192